Morning Star Paste-Up]

Cut out small swatches of your fabrics and paste them in place w..... g
ize how your finished block will look before you begin sewing.

Paper backed fusing web can also be used in place of a glue stick. Group and trace
similar designs onto a piece of fusible paper. Iron the web onto the wrong side of the
fabric, cut out the individual pieces, and peel the paper away. Iron the fabric pieces
onto the paste-up block.

A	B	A	B	A
B	A	C C	A	B
A	C C	C or D	C C	A
B	A	C C	A	B
A	B	A	B	A

A Light
Background

B Medium
Chain

C Dark
Star Points

D Dark
Star Center
(Optional)

Notions

Rotary Cutter and Gridded Board

Use a large industrial size rotary cutter capable of cutting through several layers of fabric at one time with a plexiglas ruler on a special gridded plastic mat.

Plexiglas Rulers

Use a thick 6" x 24" see-through ruler for accurately measuring and cutting strips, and a 6" x 6" ruler for squaring up the star points.

Pins

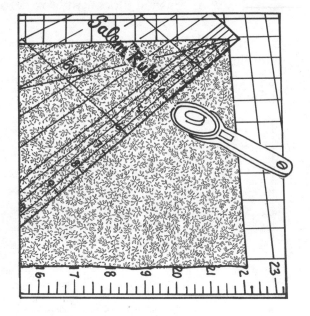

Use extra-long 1 3/4" sharp pins with the colored heads for pinning, a curved upholstery needle for tying, and #1 nickel plated safety pins for machine quilting.

Marking Pencil

Use a sharp silver pencil or sharp leaded pencil for marking your grid lines.

Presser Foot

Use a general purpose presser foot. The sewing machine needle should hit in the center of the foot. Use the edge of the foot as a guide for a 1/4" seam allowance.

Walking Foot (Optional)

An even feed foot, or walking foot, is a useful aid while machine quilting. With the walking foot, two layers of fabric and batting move together while being sewn and do not shift and become distorted.

Bicycle Clips/Trouser Bands

Wrap bicycle clips around a tightly rolled quilt when machine quilting so the quilt can fit through the "keyhole" of the machine.

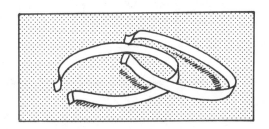

Morning Star Quilt

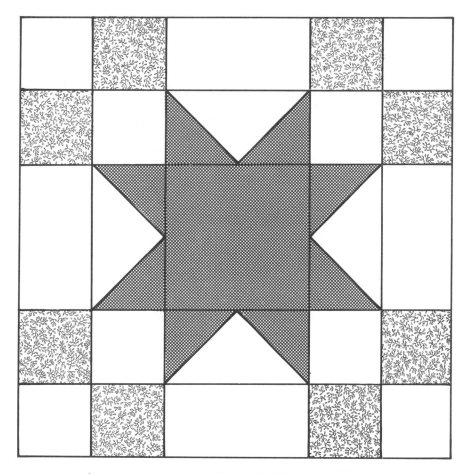

By Eleanor Burns

To Aaron - A Truly Bright Star

Illustrations and Layout by Christine Zulauf Clementi
Cover Photography by Wayne Norton, Norton Photography
Portrait Photography by Brian Steutel
Printing by A & L Litho, Escondido, Ca.

First Printing - June, 1988

Library of Congress Number 88-092069
ISBN 0-922705-12-7

Quilt in a Day® 1955 Diamond Street, Unit A   San Marcos, Ca. 92069

Table of Contents

Introduction

The most brilliant planet in the solar system, Venus, shines on us as the Morning Star! Visible three hours before sunrise from the Eastern sky, it is also know as "Lucifer" or "light bringing." Many of us enthusiatic quilters are up with that star just to catch a few short hours of "piece" and quiet before our families rise!

That very same star, the Evening Star, also known as "Hesperus," appears to us in the Western sky for three hours after sunset. What great pleasure my family and I have sharing Venus around a campfire on our southern California beach. I have fond memories of my nephew Aaron and my son Orion under the Evening Star, splashing through the ocean water in a futile search for the grunion that were to "run".

You may note the pieces in Morning Star are smaller than in some of my previous books. This calls for greater attention to accuracy in the cutting and sewing of this more intricate design. With all those tiny points to carefully match, large quilts of the Morning Star design will take you more than a day to complete - perhaps from the Morning Star to the Evening Star! But there is a definite bonus. When I laid out my first Morning Star quilt on the sewing room floor, Orion, my initial critic, exclaimed, "Oh Mom, there are so many stars! I can really see the design."

If you are new to quilting, please set *Morning Star Quilt* aside until you have gained skill and experience by making a log cabin quilt from *Quilt in a Day* or an Irish Chain quilt from *Irish Chain in a Day*. "Rusty" quilters can brush up on technique by making the Chain Blocks in the Morning Star quilt first (pages 41 to 44.) I suggest that you read the entire book first and highlight important parts. Break up your steps so your sewing is consistently accurate. Take a break in the sewing session if you begin to lose it, and come back later!

To me, the Morning Star quilt is a thing of beauty! If the Goddess Venus were here today, I just know she would enjoy making quilts! Be a Venus yourself - bring love and beauty into your home through your quilts.

Eleanor Burns

Materials and Supplies

Fabric

Select a good quality of 100% cotton 45" wide for your blocks and backing. If you wish, prewash the lights and darks separately with soap in a gentle wash cycle. If you do not prewash your fabric before making your quilt, carefully hand wash it in cold water with a delicate soap when it becomes soiled.

Batting

Select bonded polyester batting for the inside of your quilt in your choice of thicknesses. The thickest battings, 8 oz. - 10 oz., show the most dimension when tied and are the warmest. A thin batting, 2 -3 oz., is the best for hand or machine quilting. Check for a brand of bonded batting that has not been treated with formaldehyde and has no "needle drag." It should feel soft to the touch and not fall apart when tugged on. If you are going to machine quilt or "stitch in the ditch" through the borders, practice on various pieces of batting sandwiched between two pieces of fabric to find the best thickness.

Floss

Use all strands of embroidery floss, crochet thread, pearl cotton, candlewicking yarn, or 100% wool yarn for tying down the blocks. To test the durability of a fiber, hold several strands between your fingers and rub the ends briskly. Don't use yarns or fibers that fray easily. Purchase three packages of floss for sizes up to twin, and six packages for sizes through king.

Thread for the Quilt Top and Machine Quilting

Purchase a large spool of polyester spun thread in a neutral shade for sewing together the blocks and borders. Purchase an additional large spool of polyester spun thread for the bobbin to match the backing color when machine quilting or "stitching in the ditch." For machine quilting stitches that only show dimension, purchase a spool of "invisible" nylon thread in either clear or smokey for the top thread. If your quilt is light in color, select the clear; if your quilt is dark in color, select the smokey.

Color Selection and Variations

The basic Morning Star quilt uses three or four different colors of fabric.

Color A, or light, is the background color that frames the star and the connecting block.

Color B, or medium, is the chain that runs consistently throughout the quilt and connects the stars.

Color C, or dark, is a one-color star. If you wish to have a two color star, only the points of the star are Color C.

Color D, or the second dark, is the same color value as Color C and is the center of the star. It could be a large bold print, a stripe, or a one-way directional print.

One Way Prints

One way directional prints are appropriate for the medium color, or Color B, used in the connecting blocks, and Color D, the center square of the star. One way directional prints and stripes are not appropriate for Colors A and C.

Scales of Prints in the Morning Star

When you are selecting your fabrics, vary the scale of your prints for a dynamic finished look. Quilts made with fabrics using the same scale of design repeatedly tend to look boring. Choose a large scale print, a small scale print, and a solid, or one that looks like a solid from a distance.

Border Colors

The first border is generally medium to "contain" the connecting blocks and frame the quilt. The second border is generally light. The third border, backing, and optional binding is generally dark. These yardages are included in the lists. Two styles of borders are given: one with a four-patch in the corners and one with star or chain block corners.

Suggestions for Quilts with Stars of Different Colors

Plan a variation by coloring in the quilt layout stars with colored pencils. For instance, the colors of the stars could vary in each diagonal row. Consider making just two different colors of stars and place them in "checker board" fashion. The twin sized Morning Star quilt on the back cover with the pale green chain blocks and the pink and blue stars is laid out in a barn raising, or diamond design. Eleven pink stars and twelve blue stars were made for a total of twenty-three stars. The yardage, cutting, and sewing instructions were cut in half for each of the color of stars.

Cutting Instructions

Tear your fabric to put it on the straight of the grain by cutting a 1/2" nick into the selvage about 1" from the edge. Tear from one selvage to the other. If you don't get a straight edge, nick and tear again until you do.

Fold the fabric in fourths from selvage to selvage, matching the torn straight edge. It is sometimes impossible to match up the selvage sides.

Line your fabric with the grid on the board. Place the torn straight edge at zero with most of it lying to the right. Place the see-through ruler on the very edge of the fabric on the left. Line the 1/4" mark on the ruler with 1/4" of the torn straight edge. With your left hand, firmly hold the ruler.

With the rotary cutter in your right hand, begin cutting with the blade off the fabric on the mat. Put all of your strength into the rotary cutter as you cut away from you, trimming the ragged edge.

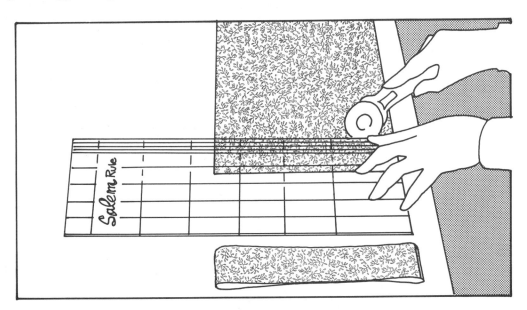

Line the edge of the fabric with zero on the gridded mat again. Move your ruler over, measuring and cutting the strips carefully and accurately from selvage to selvage. Strips will vary but most will be approximately 45" long.

If you are left-handed, reverse the cutting process with the fabric on the left and the ruler on the right.

Yardage and Cutting Charts

One Scrap Star

For a "sparkle" effect in the stars, make the centers and points of the stars all different from scrap fabrics. Use the same light background color and medium chain color throughout the quilt to "hold" it together. Find the yardage chart of your chosen size quilt for the number of stars. Under the Stars and Chains yardage column, eliminate Color C and Color D yardage if you are going to make the stars from scraps.

	Cutting Chart
Color A Light Background Same for All Stars	(1) 6" square (1) 2 1/2" x 11" strip
Color C Dark (Points)	(1) 6" square
Color C or D Dark (Center)	(1) 4 1/2" square (C or D)
Approximate Finished Size	7 3/4" Square

Pillow with Mock Ruffle

	1 Star	Cutting Chart
Color A Light Background	1/2 yd	(1) 6" square (1) 2 1/2" x 11" strip (3) 2 1/2" x 45" strips
Color B Medium Triangles	1/4 yd	(2) 6 1/2" squares
One Color Star Color C Dark (Points & Center)	7/8 yd	(3) 3 1/2" x 45" (1) 18" square (1) 6" square (4) 3 1/2" x 18" strips
Or Two Color Star Color C Dark Points And Color D Dark Center	Or 7/8 yd And 1/4 yd	Or And (1) 4 1/2" square (C or D)
Polyester Stuffing		1 bag
Bonded Batting		(2) 16" squares
Approximate Finished Size		15 1/2" Square

10

Two Pillow Shams

	6 Stars 6 Chains	Cutting Chart
Color A Light Background	3/4 yd	(4) 2 1/2" x 45" (1) 9" x 45" (1) 4 1/2" x 45"
Color B Medium Chain	3/4 yd	(2) 2 1/2" x 45" (1) 4 1/2" x 45" (6) 1 1/2" x 45"
Color C Dark (Points & Center) Or Color C Dark Points And Color D Dark Center	1 yd Or 7/8 yd And 1/4 yard	(1) 9" x 45" (6) 2 1/2" x 45" And (1) 4 1/2" x 45"
Backing – Color C or D		1 3/8 yds
Pregathered 3 1/2" Wide Lace		5 5/8 yds
Approximate Finished Size		(2) 20" x 28"

Morning Star Pillow Sham

*Morning Star Pillow
with Mock Ruffle*

Fit of the Quilts

The pattern on the finished Morning Star quilt covers the top of the bed. The first medium border frames the edge of the bed, and the borders hang over the sides. The Star Bordered Quilts are larger than the quilts with the Four Patch Corners. Check the measurements under "Approximate Finished Size" for your particular quilt. Plan to use pillow shams and a dust ruffle for the bedroom decorator look. You may need to add additional rows of blocks or borders if you want a generous tuck under the pillows and a drop to the floor. Refer to the Lover's Knot book by Eleanor Burns for instructions on making a dust ruffle.

Wallhanging or Baby Morning Star Quilt

Wallhanging or Baby Quilt

	5 Stars 4 Chains	4 Patch or Border	Star Border
Color A Light Background	2/3 yd	5/8 yd	1 3/8 yd
Color B Medium Chain	3/8 yd	3/8 yd	3/8 yd
One Color Star Color C Dark (Points & Center)	1/2 yd		7/8 yd
Or	Or	5/8 yd C or D	Or
Two Color Star Color C Dark Points and Color D Dark Center	1/3 yd and 1/4 yard		1/4 yd and 5/8 yd
Backing – Color C or D Binding (Optional)		1 1/4 yd 3/8 yd	3 yds 1/2 yd
Bonded Batting		45" sq	50" sq
Approximate Finished Size		39" x 39"	49" x 49"

Cutting Chart

	Stars and Chains	4 Patch Border	Star Border
Color A Light	(3) 2 1/2" x 45" (1) 9" x 22" (1) 4 1/2" x 22"	(5) 3 1/2" x 45"	(1) 2 1/2" x 45" (4) 8 1/4" x 45" (1) 6" x 24"
Color B Medium	(1) 2 1/2" x 45" (1) 4 1/2" x 45"	(4) 2 1/2" x 45"	(4) 2 1/2" x 45"
Color C Dark	(1) 9" x 22"		(1) 6" x 24"
Color C or Color D Dark	(1) 4 1/2" x 45"	(5) 3 1/2" x 45"	(1) 4 1/2" x 20" (4) 3 1/2" x 45"
Backing		One Piece	Two Equal Pieces
Optional Binding		(4) 2 1/2"	(5) 2 1/2"

Lap Morning Star Quilt

Lap Robe

	8 Stars 7 Chains	4 Patch or Star Border	
Color A Light Background	3/4 yd	7/8 yd	1 1/4 yd
Color B Medium Chain	3/8 yd	5/8 yd	5/8 yd
Color C Dark (Points & Center)	1/2 yd		1 1/4 yd
Or	Or	7/8 yd C or D	Or
Two Color Star Color C Dark Points And Color D Dark Center	1/3 yd And 1/4 yard		1/4 yd And 1 yd
Backing – Color C or D Binding (Optional)		1 3/4 yd 1/2 yd	3 1/4 yds 1/2 yd
Bonded Batting		45" x 60"	55" x 70"
Approximate Finished Size		43" x 58"	53" x 68"

Cutting Chart

	Stars and Chains	4 Patch Border	Star Border
Color A Light	(4) 2 1/2" x 45" (1) 9" x 45" (1) 4 1/2" x 45"	(6) 4 1/2" x 45"	(1) 2 1/2" x 45" (4) 8 1/4" x 45" (1) 6" x 24"
Color B Medium	(2) 2 1/2" x 45" (1) 4 1/2" x 45"	(4) 3 1/2" x 45"	(4) 3 1/2" x 45"
Color C Dark	(1) 9" x 45"		(1) 6" x 24"
Color C or Color D Dark	(1) 4 1/2" x 45"	(6) 4 1/2" x 45"	(1) 4 1/2" x 20" (6) 4 1/2" x 45"
Backing		One Piece	Two Equal Pieces
Optional Binding		(5) 2 1/2"	(6) 2 1/2"

Twin Morning Star Quilt

Twin Quilt

	23 Stars 22 Chains	4 Patch or Border	Star Border
Color A Light Background	2 yd	1 yd	1 3/4 yd
Color B Medium Chain	1 yd	3/4 yd	3/4 yd
One Color Star Color C Dark (Points & Center)	1 1/4 yd		1 1/2 yd
OR	OR	1 yd C or D	Or
Two Color Star Color C Dark Points and Color D Dark Center	1 yd and 1/2 yd		1/4 yd and 1 1/3 yd
Backing – Color C or D Binding (Optional)		5 1/2 yd 2/3 yd	6 yds 2/3 yd
Bonded Batting		62" x 94"	70" x 100"
Approximate Finished Size		60" x 92"	66" x 96"

Cutting Chart

	Stars and Chains	4 Patch Border	Star Border
Color A Light	(11) 2 1/2" x 45" (3) 9" x 45" (3) 4 1/2" x 45"	(7) 4 1/2" x 45"	(1) 2 1/2" x 45" (6) 8 1/4" x 45" (1) 6" x 24"
Color B Medium	(6) 2 1/2" x 45" (3) 4 1/2" x 45"	(6) 3 1/2" x 45"	(6) 3 1/2" x 45"
Color C Dark	(3) 9" x 45"		(1) 6" x 24"
Color C or Color D Dark	(3) 4 1/2" x 45"	(7) 4 1/2" x 45"	(1) 4 1/2" x 20" (8) 4 1/2" x 45"
Backing		Two Equal Pieces	Two Equal Pieces
Optional Binding		(8) 2 1/2" x 45"	(8) 2 1/2" x 45"

Double Morning Star Quilt

Double Quilt

	32 Stars 31 Chains	4 Patch or Border	Star Border
Color A Light Background	2 1/2 yd	1 1/4 yd	2 1/2 yd
Color B Medium Chain	1 1/4 yd	7/8 yd	7/8 yd
One Color Star Color C Dark (Points & Center)	1 1/2 yds		1 1/2 yd
OR	OR	1 1/4 yd C or D	Or
Two Color Star Color C Dark Points and Color D Dark Center	1 yd and 5/8 yd		1/4 yd and 1 1/3 yd
Backing – Color C or D Binding (Optional)		6 yds 2/3 yd	6 yds 2/3 yd
Bonded Batting		78" x 94"	86" x 102"
Approximate Finished Size		73" x 89"	81" x 97"

Cutting Chart

	Stars and Chains	4 Patch Border	Star Border
Color A Light	(15) 2 1/2" x 45" (3) 9" x 45" (4) 4 1/2" x 45" (1) 3" x 6"	(8) 4 1/2" x 45"	(1) 2 1/2" x 45" (9) 8 1/4" x 45" (1) 6" x 24"
Color B Medium	(8) 2 1/2" x 45" (4) 4 1/2" x 45"	(7) 3 1/2" x 45"	(7) 3 1/2" x 45"
Color C Dark	(3) 9" x 45" (1) 3" x 6"	(8) 4 1/2" x 45"	(1) 6" x 24"
Color C or Color D Dark	(4) 4 1/2" x 45"		(1) 4 1/2" x 20" (9) 4 1/2" x 45"
Backing		Two Equal Pieces	Two Equal Pieces
Optional Binding		(8) 2 1/2" x 45"	(8) 2 1/2" x 45"

Queen Morning Star Quilt

Queen Quilt

	32 Stars 31 Chains	4 Patch or Border	Star Border
Color A Light Background	2 1/2 yd	1 1/2 yd	2 1/2 yd
Color B Medium Chain	1 1/4 yd	1 yd	1 yd
One Color Star Color C Dark (Points & Center)	1 1/2 yds		1 3/4 yd
OR	OR	1 1/2 yd C or D	Or
Two Color Star Color C Dark Points and Color D Dark Center	1 yd and 5/8 yard		1/4 yd and 1 5/8 yd
Backing – Color C or D Binding (Optional)		6 yds 3/4 yd	6 yds 3/4 yd
Bonded Batting		84" x 100"	86" x 102"
Approximate Finished Size		78" x 94"	84" x 100"

Cutting Chart

	Stars and Chains	4 Patch Border	Star Border
Color A Light	(15) 2 1/2" x 45" (3) 9" x 45" (4) 4 1/2" x 45" (1) 3" x 6"	(9) 5 1/2" x 45"	(1) 2 1/2" x 45" (9) 8 1/4" x 45" (1) 6" x 24"
Color B Medium	(8) 2 1/2" x 45" (4) 4 1/2" x 45"	(7) 4 1/2" x 45"	(7) 4 1/2" x 45"
Color C Dark	(3) 9" x 45" (1) 3" x 6"	(9) 5 1/2" x 45"	(1) 6" x 24"
Color C or Color D Dark	(4) 4 1/2" x 45"		(1) 4 1/2" x 20" (9) 5 1/2" x 45"
Backing		Two Equal Pieces	Two Equal Pieces
Optional Binding		(9) 2 1/2" x 45"	(9) 2 1/2" x 45"

King Morning Star Quilt

King Quilt

	50 Stars 49 Chains	4 Patch Border	or Star Border
Color A Light Background	4 yds	1 3/4 yd	2 1/2 yd
Color B Medium Chain	2 yds	1 1/4 yd	1 1/4 yd
One Color Star Color C Dark (Points & Center)	2 1/4 yds		2 1/4 yd
Or	Or	1 3/4 yd C or D	Or
Two Color Star Color C Dark Points and Color D Dark Center	1 1/3 yd and 1 yd		1/4 yd and 2 yds
Backing – Color C or D Binding (Optional)		8 1/2 yds 1 yd	9 yds 1 yd
Bonded Batting		98" x 113"	104" x 119"
Approximate Finished Size		93" x 108"	99" x 115"

Cutting Chart

	Stars and Chains	4 Patch Border	Star Border
Color A Light	(25) 2 1/2" x 45" (5) 9" x 45" (6) 4 1/2" x 45"	(10) 5 1/2" x 45"	(1) 2 1/2" x 45" (9) 8 1/4" x 45" (1) 6" x 24"
Color B Medium	(12) 2 1/2" x 45" (6) 4 1/2" x 45"	(8) 4 1/2" x 45"	(8) 4 1/2" x 45"
Color C Dark	(5) 9" x 45"		(1) 6" x 24"
Color C or Color D Dark	(6) 4 1/2" x 45"	(10) 5 1/2" x 45"	(1) 4 1/2" x 20" (11) 5 1/2" x 45"
Backing		Three Pieces	Three Pieces
Optional Binding		(11) 2 1/2" x 45"	(12) 2 1/2" x 45"

Basic Construction of Morning Star Quilt

There are two basic pieces that go into the completed Morning Star Quilt: the star block and the chain block.

Star Block

The **Star Block** is comprised of **Section 1** and **Section 2**. **Section 1** is used twice in the block. It consists of light corners (A) and dark points (C). **Section 2** is used once in the block. It consists of a dark center (C or D) and dark points (C).

Number per Quilt   Baby - 5
Lap - 8
Twin - 23
Double - 32
Queen - 32
King - 50

Pillow - 1
Star Border - 4
Pillow Shams - 6

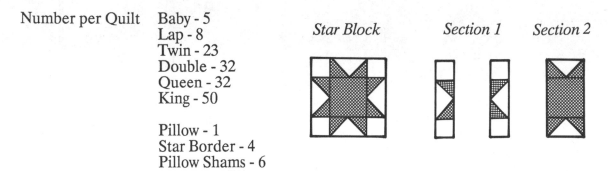

Star Block   *Section 1*   *Section 2*

Chain Block

The **Chain Block** is comprised of **Section 3** and **Section 4**. **Section 3** is used twice in the block. It consists of a light strip (A) and medium squares (B). **Section 4** is used once in the block. It consists of a medium center (B) and light strips (A).

Number per Quilt   Baby - 4
Lap - 7
Twin - 22
Double - 31
Queen - 31
King - 49

Pillow - 0
Star Border - 0
Pillow Shams - 6

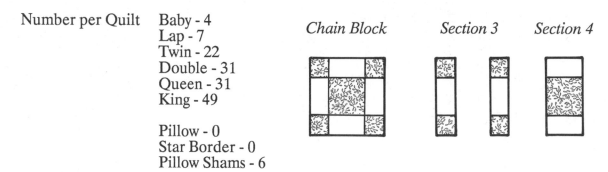

Chain Block   *Section 3*   *Section 4*

The instructions in Morning Star feature a dark star and a medium chain block. If you have done any color variations, please pencil in your changes by the illustrations.

This is an example of a Baby Quilt layout with the Star Blocks and Chain Blocks.

Sewing Accurately

1/4" Seam Allowance

Use a 1/4" seam allowance throughout your sewing. Two tools, the proper presser foot and a magnetic seam guide, can assist you in sewing accurately and consistently.

Check Your 1/4" seam allowance.

The easiest way to check the width on your seam allowance is to sew on a piece of lined notebook paper without thread. Follow along a line with the edge of your presser foot. Measure the width of the seam. Change presser feet or make an adjustment in your sewing for a 1/4" seam.

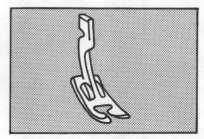

presser foot

Because of the sewing method used for making the points in the star, an overlock sewing machine should not be used for the Star Block. Once the points are sewn, a magnetic seam guide can be used on any machine with a metal throat plate, other than the computerized machines. Carefully measure the distance from the needle to the edge of seam guide for a 1/4" seam. When you sew, line up the edge of the pieces against the magnet.

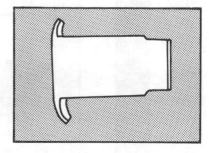

magnetic seam guide

Option of using an Overlock for sewing the Chain Block.

The overlock may be used for making the Chain Block. Use the identical 1/4" seam allowance when sewing with the second machine, in order that the Star Block and the Chain Block will fit together and match perfectly in the finished quilt.

15 Stitches Per Inch

Set your machine at the tight stitch, 15 stitches per inch, or a #2 on machines with stitch selections from #1 - #4. This tight stitch is used because backstitching is rarely done in assembly line sewing.

Making the Points of the Star

1. Place the 9" strips of light (Color A) and dark (Color C) right sides together. Press.

2. Position the gridded cutting mat so that zero is in the left hand bottom corner. Place the edge of the 9" strips on the gridded cutting mat in that corner.

3. Trim the selvage edges on the left side.

4. Draw on perpendicular lines every 3" following the grid according to your particular size quilt. Cut off any excess.

Draw on 3" horizontal lines.

For instance, a baby quilt needs a 9" x 21" piece. Draw on 3" perpendicular lines to 21". Cut at 21". Draw on horizontal lines every 3".

Number Per Quilt

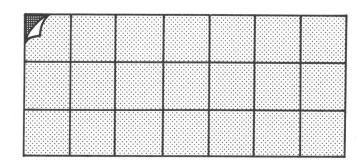

Baby Quilt -	(1) 9" x 21"			
Lap Robe -	(1) 9" x 21"			
	(1) 9 x 12"			

Twin Quilt -	(4) 9" x 21"	Queen Quilt -	(6) 9" x 21"			
	(1) 9" x 9"		(1) 3" x 6"	One Star Block -	6" x 6"	
				Star Border -	9" x 15"	
Double Quilt -	(6) 9" x 21"	King Quilt -	(9) 9" x 21"	Pillow Shams -	(1) 9" x 21"	
	(1) 3" x 6"		(1) 9" x 12"		(1) 6" x 6"	

These sizes of pieces are designed for sewing ease. Additional smaller pieces are included to assist your in reaching your total number of points needed. Draw a 3" grid on them also.

Example of a 3" x 6" rectangle (used in the Double and Queen):

Example of a 6" square (used when making only one star):

The 21" cut is made near the fold. The fold can be eliminated on larger quilts.

5. Draw on diagonal lines **starting in the marked corner** every other row.

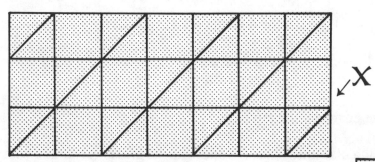

Example of a 3" x 6" rectangle (used in the Double and Queen):

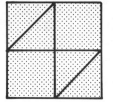

Example of a 6" square (used when making only one star):

6. Draw on diagonal lines in the opposite direction in the empty rows that are left.

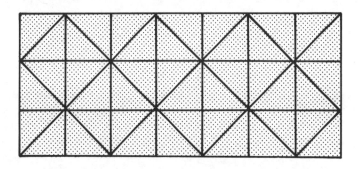

                                                                    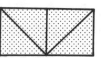

Example of a 3" x 6" rectangle (used in the Double and Queen):

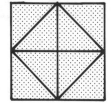

Example of a 6" square (used when making only one star):

Sewing 1/4" from these diagonal lines is extremely important. To help you get started with your sewing, find the long 1/4" line marked along the edge of your ruler.

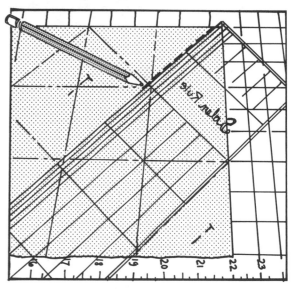

7. Place this 1/4" line on top of your drawn line in the upper right corner. Draw a dashed sewing line through two of the blocks 1/4" away from the solid line. **This is your guide line for sewing.**

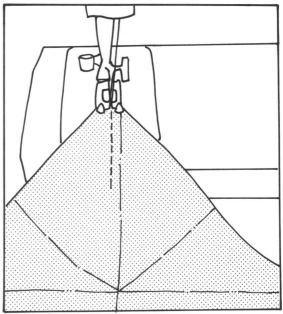

8. **Pin the two pieces together** in the center of the "diamonds."

9. Begin sewing on the dashed sewing line. Maintain this seam allowance throughout your sewing. Depending on the width of your presser foot, you may line up the edge of the foot with the diagonal line.

It is better to have a generous 1/4" seam rather than a skimpy one!

If the stitching line is a few threads over 1/4", the finished star will fit together better than if the seam was a few threads less than 1/4".

10. At the end of the first line, turn the strip and continue sewing 1/4" from the diagonal line. Pivot the strip with the needle in the fabric at the grid lines.

11. Continuously sew, pivoting the fabric until you reach the left hand corner and can not sew any further. Turn the piece around.

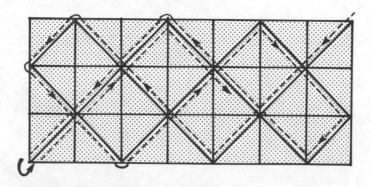

12. Sew on the other side of the diagonal line. Do not backstitch.

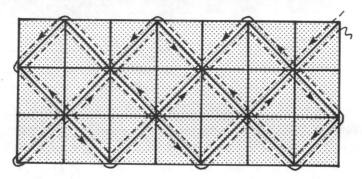

13. Press.

14. Lay the stitched piece on the cutting board. Line it up with the grid. With the rotary cutter and ruler, cut apart on the 3" square lines. Cut apart on all the diagonal lines exactly as you marked them.

If you leave the piece lying flat on the board, you can make long diagonal cuts, and cut them apart very quickly.

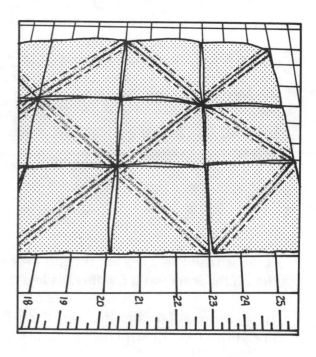

30

Pressing Your Seams to the Dark Side

Use steam at a cotton setting on your iron.

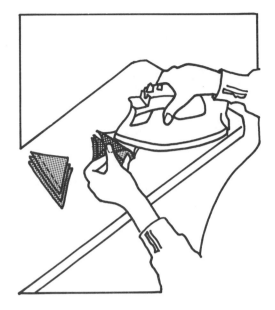

1. Stack the pieces into several piles. Do not open up the pieces. Place the piles on the ironing board with light sides on the bottom.

2. Drop one piece in the center of the ironing board with the light on the bottom.

3. Lift up the dark part and press it open and flat. Do not put down the iron.

4. Lay a second piece on top of the first with light side down again. Press it open and flat.

5. Continue to press without putting down the iron; stack as you press the pieces. The dark and light will always be in the same position.

You should have a total of this many pieces

Baby - 40
Lap - 64
Twin - 184
Double - 256
Queen - 256
King - 400

One Star Block - 8
Star Border - 32
Pillow Shams - 48

Approximate Size: 2 1/2" square

Sewing the Points into Pairs

1. Sort into two equal piles with this many per pile

Baby - 20
Lap - 32
Twin - 92
Double - 128
Queen - 128
King - 200

One Star Bock - 4
Star Border - 16
Pillow Shams - 24

(Piles can be approximate for the larger size quilts. If the 3" grid marking was done correctly, there will be the correct number. When you assembly line sew them together, just sew until all pieces are sewn into pairs.)

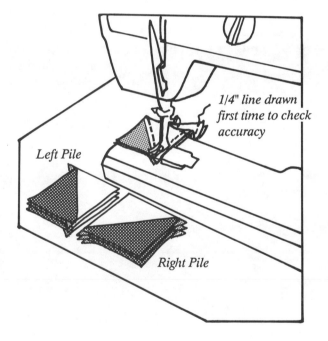

Left Pile

1/4" line drawn first time to check accuracy

Right Pile

2. Lay them in this order near your sewing machine.

3. Place a magnetic seam guide on the throat plate of your sewing machine 1/4" away from the needle.

4. Flip the piece on the right onto the piece on the left, right sides together. To check your seam allowance this first time, draw on a dashed line 1/4" from the raw edges.

5. Sew them together. Check to see that your 1/4" seam is accurate.

6. Assembly line sew all the remaining pairs together.

Follow this procedure:

Flip the piece on the right onto the piece on the left, right sides together. Match the top edges and the tips. Open them up at the bottom edge to make certain that the diagonal lines match.

Stitch. Do not remove the piece from the machine.

Flip the second set of pieces right sides together. Check to see that they match. Butt the second set onto the first without raising the presser foot or clipping the threads.

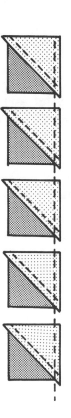

Pressing the Points of the Star

1. Lay the long chain of points on the ironing board in the exact order as shown in the illustration. The seam is pressed in the right direction for the next sewing steps. Do not press the seam open.

2. Fold back the first block and press. Fold back the second and press. Continue to open each one and press.

3. Cut them apart. Stack in one pile.

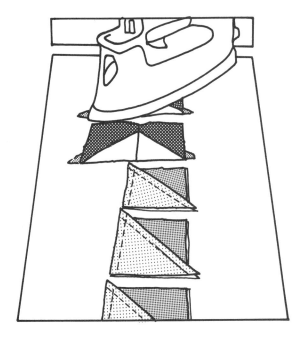

Squaring Up the Pairs of Points to 2 1/2" x 4 1/2"

Do not skip this step! It is a time consuming, but vital step necessary in making points that match on the stars.

The 6" square mini ruler and rotary cutter are the most convenient tools for this "squaring up" step.

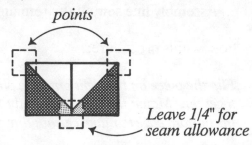

points

Leave 1/4" for seam allowance

1. Lay the 6" square mini ruler on top of one pair of points. The center seam on the points should line up with the 2 1/4" mark on the ruler. The quarter inch seam allowance line should line up with the stitched "V".

Adjust the ruler so that the points are not cut off.

2. Trim off any excess fabric around the edge of the ruler.

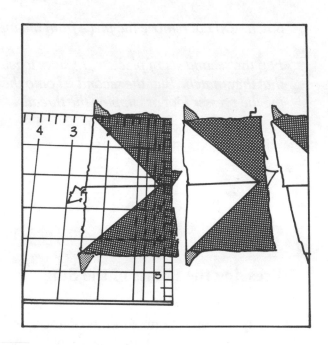

3. Turn the pair of points around. Line up the center seam with the 2 1/4" line on the ruler.

4. Trim off excess fabric.

Be careful not to lose your points or seam allowance when trimming.

5. Repeat the "squaring up" process for each pair.

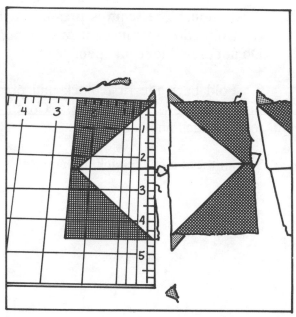

Making Section 1 - The Light Squares and Dark Points

Section 1 is used twice in the Star Block.

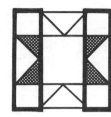

1. Count out this many 2 1/2" x 45" light strips (Color A) for your particular quilt size:

Baby - 2 strips	One Star Block - (1) 11" strip
Lap - 2 strips	Star Border - 1 strip
Twin - 6 strips	Pillow Shams - 2 strips
Double - 8 strips	
Queen - 8 strips	
King - 14 strips	

Square off one end on all strips. Start sewing at this end.

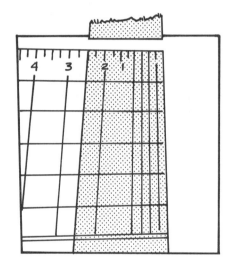

2. Divide into two equal piles.

3. **Count out half of your dark point pairs** for your particular size quilt

Baby - 10	
Lap - 16	One Star Block - 2
Twin - 46	Star Border - 8
Double - 64	Pillow Shams - 12
Queen - 64	
King - 100	

Set aside the extra points for Section 2.

4. Lay one pile of light strips and dark point pairs in this order:

5. Place the dark point pair right sides together to the light strip.

6. Stitch.

7. Butt the second dark point pair right sides together to the light strip after the first pair. Stitch.

8. Sew all point pairs onto the light strips. Start a new strip when the last section of the light strip is less than 2 1/2".

9. Square off the ends of the strips after the last point pair is added.

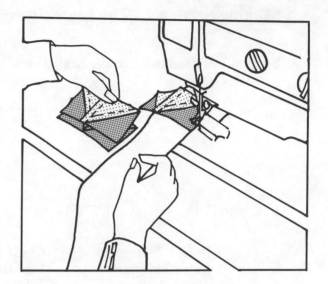

10. *Turn the strips around so that the last point you sewed is at the top.* With the second pile, continue to stitch light strips to the other side of the point pairs.

Start a new strip if you can not fit the point pair onto the end of the strip.

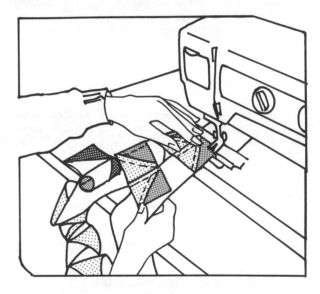

11. Drop Section 1 right side up on the ironing board. Open the light strips and press so that the seams lie behind the light strips.

12. Cut the point pairs apart on the light strips only. The cuts will be approximately every 2 1/2".

13. Stack into two equal piles.

14. Set aside until Section 2 is completed.

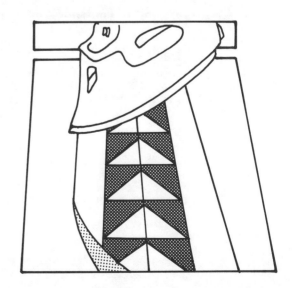

Making Section 2 - The Center Strip of the Star Block

Section 2 is used once in the Star Block.

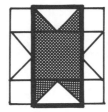

1. Count out this many 4 1/2" strips of the dark (Color C or D) for your particular size quilt:

Baby - 1 strip
Lap - 1 strip
Twin - 3 strips
Double - 4 strips   One Star Block - (1) 4 1/2" square
Queen - 4 strips   Star Border - 1/2 strip
King - 6 strips   Pillow Shams - 1 strip

2. Square off one end of each of the strips. Start sewing at this end.

3. Count out two equal stacks of dark points.

Place this many in each stack.

Baby - 5   One Star Block - 1
Lap - 8   Star Border - 4
Twin - 23   Pillow Shams - 6
Double - 32
Queen - 32
King - 50

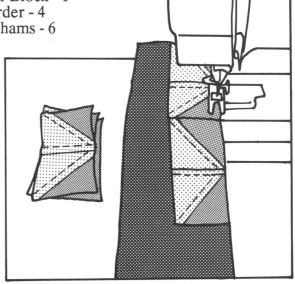

4. Place one stack of points right sides down and the 4 1/2" strips right side up in this order at your sewing machine.

5. Assembly line sew the dark points to one side of the dark strips by butting the points closely together, but not overlapping them.

Check your first couple of blocks from the right side for sharp points.

If it appears that your 1/4" stitching line will "cut off" the bottom of the point, pull that middle section to the left slightly so that the stitching hits right on the bottom of the points.

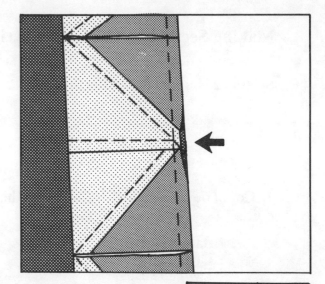

6. Start a new strip if the last part of the strip is less than 4 1/2".

7. Square off excess parts of the strips.

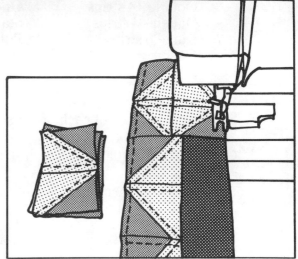

8. Reverse the strips so that the bottom is now at the top.

9. Sew the points to the opposite side of the strip. **The points on the second side must be straight across from the points on the first side.**

Pressing Section 2

1. Lay the 4 1/2" strip on the ironing board with the wide strip right sides down.

2. Pull out the points from under the strip.

3. Press the seams toward the 4 1/2" strip.

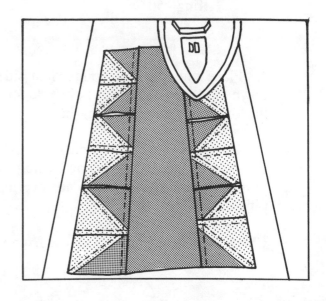

Cutting Apart Section Two

1. With the rotary cutter and ruler, cut apart between the two points.

2. Stack in one pile.

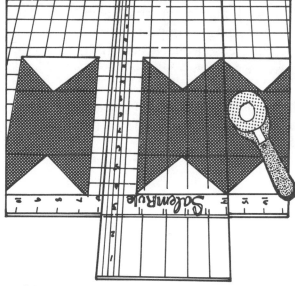

Sewing the Star Block Together

1. Lay out two stacks of Section 1 and one stack of Section 2 with the dark center square in this order:

Place this many in each stack

Baby - 5
Lap - 8
Twin - 23
Double - 32
Queen - 32
King - 50

One Star Block - 1
Star Border - 4
Pillow Shams - 6

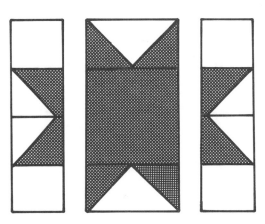

2. Flip #1 on the right together to #2. Match the top edges. Anchor the two pieces together by stitching down 1/4".

3. Match and fingerpin the first seam. The seams are going in opposite directions. Stretch or ease as necessary to fit. Stitch across the seam.

4. Match and fingerpin the second seam. Stretch or ease. Stitch to the end of the block, matching the seams.

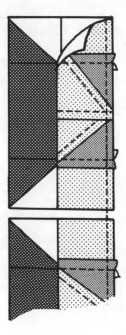

5. Repeat with the second set of #1's and #2's, butting them behind the first set.

Continue until all #1's are sewn onto #2's.

6. Flip the star block around so that last star is now at the top.

7. Add the second pile of #1's to #2's in the same assembly line order.

8. Press.

9. Cut apart. Stack in one pile and set aside until Block 2 completed.

Making The Chain Block

Making Section 3 with Light and Medium Strips

Section 3 is used twice in the Connecting Block.

1. Place the 4 1/2" light strips (Color A) between two stacks of 2 1/2" strips medium (Color B) in this order:

Place this many strips in each stack

Baby - 1/2
Lap - 1
Twin - 3
Double - 4
Queen - 4
King - 6

Pillow Shams - 1

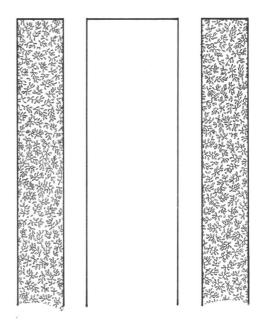

2. Seam the strips together lengthwise with an accurate 1/4" seam allowance. Use a magnetic seam guide for accuracy.

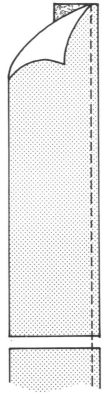

3. Place Section 3 on the ironing board with the 4 1/2" light strip right side up. Open and press the seams to the medium side.

4. Place Section 3 on a gridded board.

5. Square off one end.

6. Cut apart into 2 1/2" sections.

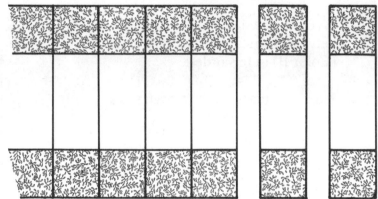

Cut this many for your quilt

        Baby - 8
        Lap - 14
        Twin - 44
        Double - 62
        Queen - 62
        King - 98

        Pillow Shams - 12

7. Stack into two equal piles.

8. Set aside until Section 4 is completed.

Making Section 4

Section 4 is used once in the Chain Block.

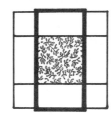

1. Place the 4 1/2" medium strip (Color B) between two 2 1/2" light strips (Color A) in this order:

Place this many in each stack

> Baby - 1/2 strip
> Lap - 1 strip
> Twin - 2 1/2 strip
> Double - 3 1/2 strips
> Queen - 3 1/2 strips
> King - 5 1/2 strips
>
> Pillow Shams - 1 strip

2. Seam together lengthwise.

3. Open up Section 4 and place right sides down on the ironing board. Press the seams to the medium side.

4. Square off one end.

5. Cut into 4 1/2" sections.

Cut this many for your quilt

> Baby - 4
> Lap - 7
> Twin - 22
> Double - 31
> Queen - 31
> King - 49
>
> Pillow Shams - 6

7. Stack in one pile.

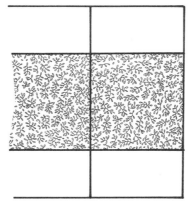

Sewing The Chain Block Together

1. Lay out two piles of Section 3 and one pile of Section 4 in this order:

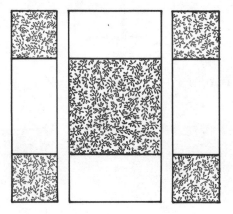

2. Assembly line sew them together, matching each of the seams. Push the seams in the same direction they were pressed.

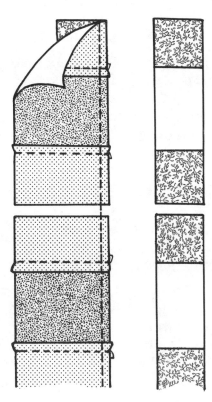

3. Place the chain blocks wrong side up on the ironing board. Press the medium toward the center.

4. Cut apart.

Sewing the Blocks Together

Laying Out Your Quilt

1. Lay out your selected size quilt in a large area following the corresponding illustration.

Alternate between the Star Block and the Chain Block, beginning and ending with the Star Blocks in the corners. Begin each row with the opposite of the block beside it.

Number of Blocks Across and Down

Shams - 2 x 3

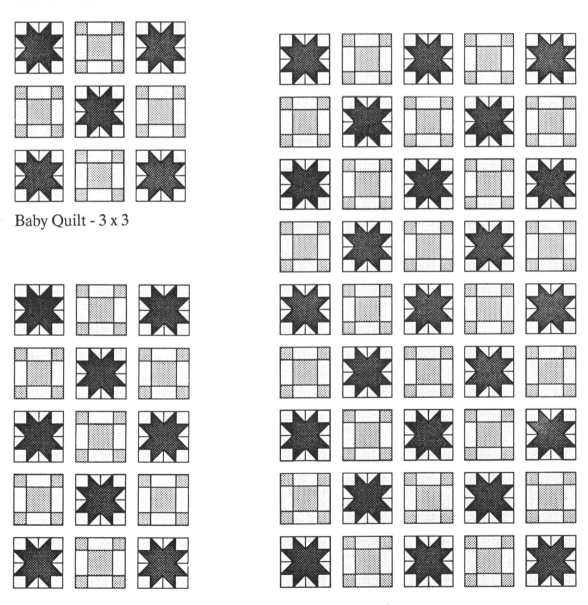

Baby Quilt - 3 x 3

Lap Robe - 3 x 5   Twin Quilt - 5 x 9

Double Quilt - 7 x 9

Queen Quilt - 7 x 9

King Quilt - 9 x 11

2. Flip the second vertical row right sides together onto the first vertical row.

3. Pick up the pairs of blocks in the first vertical row from the bottom to the top. The pair of blocks at the top will be on the top of the stack.

4. Stack up each one of the vertical rows from the bottom to the top, having the top block on the top of the stack each time.

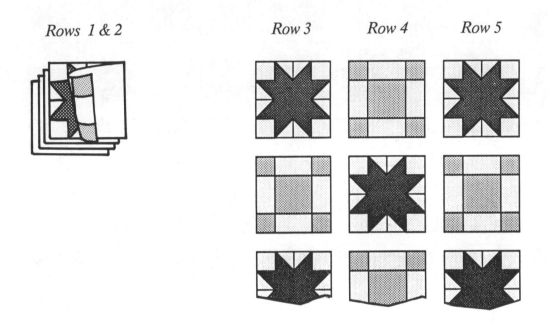

Rows 1 & 2　　　*Row 3*　　*Row 4*　　*Row 5*

5. Write the row number on a small piece of paper and pin it through all thicknesses of fabric.

Example Illustration: Your quilt may have a different number of rows.

Sewing the First Two Vertical Rows

1. Start in the upper left hand corner. Pick up the Star Block and the Chain Block right sides together from Rows 1 and 2.

2. Match the outside edges of the blocks. Backstitch, and stitch down about 1/2" to anchor the two together.

3. Match and fingerpin by squeezing tightly the first point of the star and the square on the chain. Stitch across the match point.

4. Match and fingerpin the second point of the star and the square on the chain. Ease or stretch the pieces to meet. Stitch across the match point.

5. Match the outside edges of the block and stitch.

Do not cut the threads or lift the presser foot.

6. Pick up the next pair of blocks. Butt them right behind the first two.

7. Anchor the two. Match, fingerpin, and stitch as in the previous pair of blocks.

8. Continue butting on all star and chain blocks in the same manner until the two rows are completed.

9. Backstitch on the very last edge.

Do not cut the blocks apart.

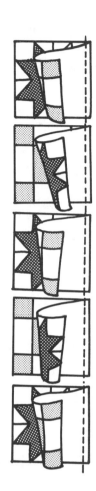

Sewing the Third Vertical Row

1. Place the star block at the top of the third vertical row right sides together to the chain block at the top of the second vertical row.

2. Anchor, match, fingerpin, and stitch.

3. Butt on the next chain block. Anchor, match, fingerpin, and stitch.

Continue to sew on all blocks in the third vertical row and all remaining rows in this manner.

Do not clip the threads holding the blocks together.

Example Illustration: Yours may look different according to the size of quilt.

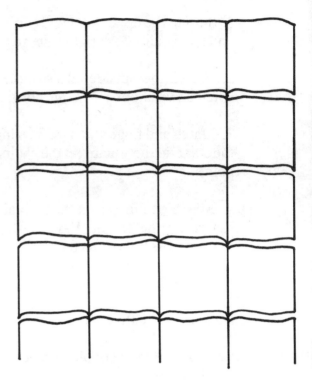

Sewing the Horizontal Rows

1. Flip the top row down onto the second row with right sides together.

2. Match, fingerpin, and stitch the blocks to meet. Where the two blocks are joined by a thread from stitching in the vertical rows, match the seam carefully. Push one seam allowance up on one side, and one down on the other side.

3. Stitch all horizontal rows in the same manner.

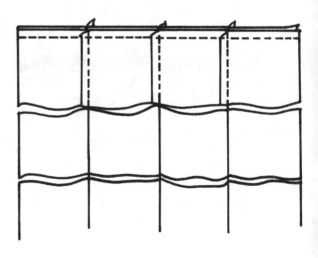

Adding the Borders to your Quilt

If you wish to custom fit the quilt, lay the quilt top out on your bed before you add the borders and backing. Measure to find how much border you need to get the fit you want. Keep in mind that the quilt will "shrink" approximately 4" in the length and width after completion of tying, "stitching in the ditch," and/or machine quilting.

Piecing the Borders

1. Follow the Individual Cutting Charts for the widths of each border cut from selvage to selvage.

2. Seam the strips of each color into long pieces by flashfeeding. Lay the first strip right side up. Lay the second strip right sides to it. Backstitch, stitch the short ends together, and backstitch again.

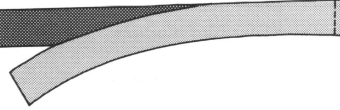

3. Take the strip on the top and fold it so the right side is up.

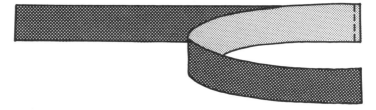

4. Place the third strip right sides to it, backstitch, stitch, and backstitch again.

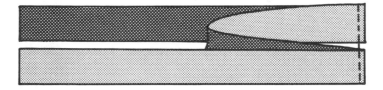

5. Continue flashfeeding all the short ends together into long pieces for each color.

6. Clip the threads holding the strips together.

Adding the First Border of Medium Color B to the Quilt Top

1. Measure the long sides of the quilt. Cut two pieces of Color B the same length.

2. Pin the borders to the long sides.

3. Stitch. Fold them out flat.

4. Measure the short sides of the quilt from one outside edge to the other, including the borders.

5. Cut two borders of that measurement.

6. Pin the borders to the short sides.

7. Stitch. Fold them out flat.

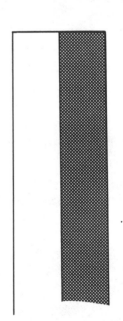

Border with the Four Patch Corners

Sewing the Light Color A and Dark Color C or D Together

1. Place the two long strips right sides together.

2. Stitch the length of the two strips.

3. Press the seams to the dark side.

Making the Four Patch Corners

1. Cut eight sections off one end.

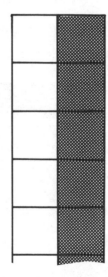

Baby - (8) 3 1/2" sections
Lap, Twin, and Double - (8) 4 1/2" sections
Queen and King - (8) 5 1/2" sections

2. Divide into two equal piles with 4 sections in each stack.

3. Arrange them in this order: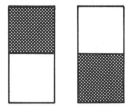

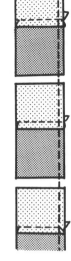

4. Assembly line sew the "four patches" together, matching the center seams.

5. Press. Snip the threads holding them together.

Star Border

1. Complete the four stars following the instructions on pages 27 to 40.

Adding the Next Borders for Both the Star and Four Patch Corners

1. Measure the long sides of the quilt. Cut two border pieces the same length in the 8 1/4" Color A strips for the Star Border or the sewn together strips of Colors A/C for the Four Patch Border.

2. Measure the short sides of the quilt. Cut two border pieces the same length.

3. Pin the two long border pieces to the two long sides of the quilt top with right sides together. Sew. Unfold.

4. Sew a star or "four patch" to each end of the two short border strips.

5. Pin and sew these strips onto each short end of the quilt.

Star Border Only

1. Add the last border of Color C or D in the same manner.

Finishing the Quilt

Two different methods are given for finishing the Morning Star Quilt

Quick Turn Method: The first method, the Quick Turn method, is the easiest and fastest method of finishing the quilt. Thick batting is "rolled" into the middle of the quilt, and the layers are held together with ties. Borders may be "stitched in the ditch" for additional dimension. (Pages 55- 58)

Machine Quilting and Binding: In the second method, the three layers of backing, batting, and quilt top are machine quilted and bound with a straight grain strip of binding. A thin batting is generally used so that the quilt looks "old fashioned." (Pages 59 - 60)

Preparing the Backing Fabric and Batting for Either Method

1. Following the individual Cutting Charts, fold and cut the backing into equal pieces.

2. Tear off the selvages and seam the backing pieces together.

Piecing the Bonded Batting

The batting may need to be pieced to get the desired size.

1. Cut the batting. Butt the two edges closely together without overlapping.

2. Whipstitch the edges together with a double strand of thread. Do not pull the threads tightly as this will create a hard ridge visible on the outside of the quilt.

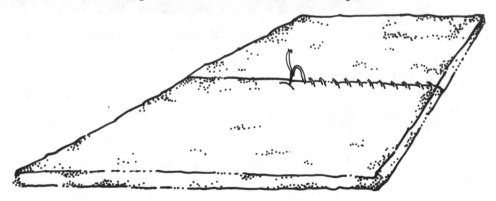

Quick Turn Method

1. Lay out the backing fabric on a large table or floor area with right side up.

2. Lay the quilt top on the backing fabric with right sides together. Stretch and smooth out the top. Pin. Trim away excess fabric. They should be the same size.

3. Stitch around the four sides of the quilt, leaving a 24 inch opening in the middle of one long side. **Do not turn the quilt right side out.**

4. Lay the quilt on top of the batting. Smooth and trim the batting to the same size as the quilt top.

5. To assure that the batting stays out to the edges, quickly whipstitch the batting to the 1/4" seam allowance around the outside edge of the quilt.

Turning the Quilt Top

This part of making your quilt is particularly exciting. One person can turn the quilt alone, but it's fun to turn it into a 10-minute family or neighborhood event with three or four others. **Read this whole section before beginning.**

1. If you are working with a group, station the people at the corners of the quilt. If working alone, start in one corner opposite the opening.

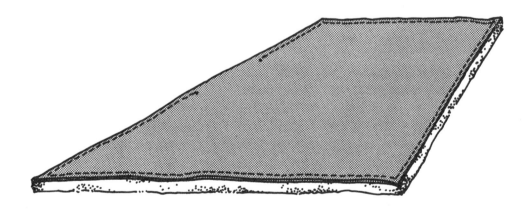

2. Roll the corners and sides tightly to keep the batting in place as you roll toward the opening.

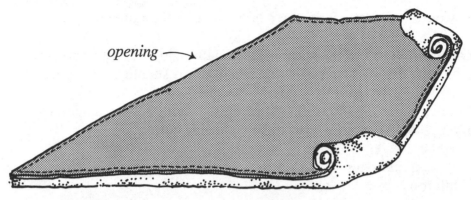

opening →

If several people are helping, all should roll toward the opening. If only one is doing the rolling, use a knee to hold down one corner while stretching over to the other corners.

3. Open up the opening over this huge wad of fabric and batting and pop the quilt right side out through the hole.

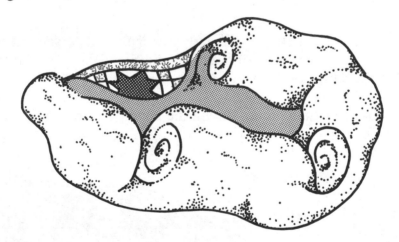

4. Unroll carefully with the layers together.

5. Lay the quilt flat on the floor or on a very large table. Work out all wrinkles and bumps by stationing two people opposite each other around the quilt. Have each person grasp the edge and tug the quilt in opposite directions.

6. You can also relocate any batting by reaching inside the quilt through the opening with a yardstick. Hold the edges and shake the batting into place if necessary.

7. Slipstitch the opening shut.

Finishing the Quick Turn Quilt

You may choose to tie your quilt down, machine quilt it with a "stitch in the ditch" technique, or use a combination of both by tying down the blocks and "stitching in the ditch" around the borders.

Tying the Quilt

1. Thread a large-eyed curved needle with a long strand of wool yarn, embroidery floss, or crochet thread.

If you want your square knot to show, use wool yarn. If the knot detracts from the look you want, use floss or crochet thread. For an invisible tie on the right side, pin all the points on the right side, flip the quilt to the wrong side, and tie at all pin marks.

2. With your fingers, poke in and plan where you want your ties placed. You may choose to tie just the corners of the chain block, or also tie parts of the star for a more dimensional look.

3. Starting in the center of the quilt and working to the outside squares, take a 1/4" stitch through all thicknesses at the points you wish to tie. Draw the needle along to each point, going in and out, and replacing the tying material as you need it.

Do not tie the borders down if you wish to "stitch in the ditch."

4. Clip all the stitches midway.

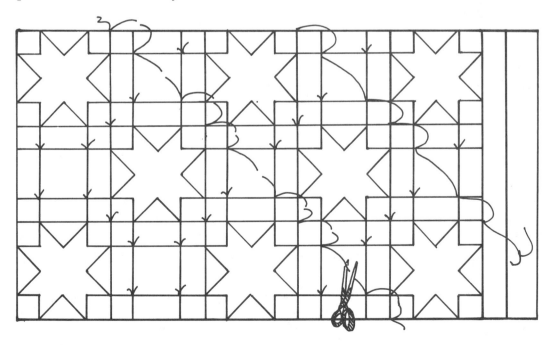

5. Tie the strands into surgeon's square knots by taking the strand on the right and wrapping it twice. Pull the knot tight. Take the strand on the left, wrap it twice, and pull the knot twice.

6. Clip the strands so they are 1/2" to 1" long.

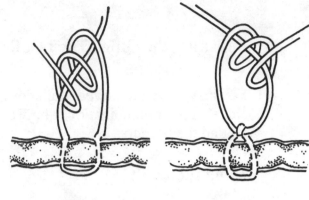

Right over left.
Wrap twice.
Pull tight.

Left over right.
Wrap twice.
Pull tight.

Stitching in the Ditch

For more dimensional borders, you may choose to "stitch in the ditch" around borders rather than tie them.

1. Change your stitch length to 10 stitches per inch. Match your bobbin color of thread to your backing color.

Loosen the top tension and thread the soft nylon invisible thread on the top. (As you sew, watch that this light thread does not drop down and wrap around the thread post as you stitch. Feeding the thread from above with the use of a high thread strand prevents this.)

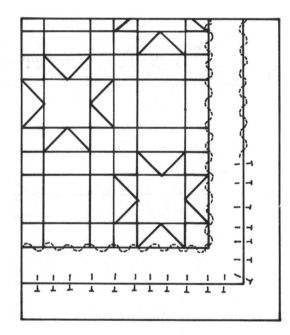

2. Change your stitch to a serpentine stitch if available and desired. This stitch does not need to be as accurately stitched in the ditch as the straight stitch to look attractive. Quite often, this is the stitch used by manufacturers for machine quilting.

3. Pin "across the ditch" the length of the borders.

4. Place the needle in the depth of the seam and stitch. Avoid puckering on the back of the quilt by running your hand underneath to feel for puckers, grasping the quilt with your left hand above the sewing machine foot, grasping the quilt with your right hand ten inches below the sewing machine foot, and stretching between the two as you stitch.

To avoid further puckering on the back, you may choose to use an even feed foot or walking foot, available for most sewing machines.

Machine Quilting

1. Lightly mark diagonal lines through the chain blocks with a silver pencil or a hard, sharp sliver of soap.

2. Stretch out the backing right side down on a large floor area or table. Tape down on a floor area or clamp onto a table. Large binder clips are excellent as clamps for tables.

3. Place the batting on top. Lay the quilt top right side up on top of the batting. Completely smooth and stretch all layers until they are flat.

4. Pin safety pins every 5" throughout the quilt away from the diagonal stitching lines.

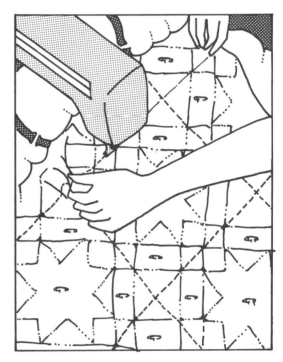

5. Trim the backing and batting to within 2" of the outside edge of the quilt.

6. Roll the quilt tightly from the outside edge in toward the middle on the diagonal. Hold this roll with metal bicycle clips or pins.

7. Slide this roll into the keyhole of the the sewing machine.

8. Using the same machine set up and technique as described on page 58, sew down the long diagonal lines. Work from the center out to the outside edge. Unroll and re-roll the quilt as necessary to get all the marked lines stitched.

Adding the Binding To Your Machine Quilted Quilt

1. Assembly line sew the 2 1/2" x 45" binding strips into one long strip.

> **Continue to use 10 stitches per inch.**
> **Your thread should match your binding and backing.**
> **Use an even feed foot, if available.**

2. Press in half lengthwise with right sides out. Turn under a 1/2" hem and press on the narrow end of the binding strip.

3. Begin applying the binding to the middle of one long side. Match the raw edge of the binding strip right sides together to the raw edge of the quilt.

Making the Mitered Corner

1. At the corner, stop the stitching 1/4" from the edge with the needle in the fabric. Raise the presser foot and turn the quilt to the next side. Put the foot back down.

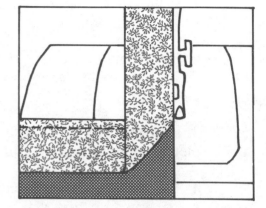

2. Stitch backwards 1/4", raise the presser foot, and pull the quilt forward slightly.

3. Fold the binding strip straight up on the diagonal. Fingerpress in the diagonal fold.

4. Fold the binding strip straight down with the diagonal fold underneath. Line up the top of the fold with the raw edge of the binding underneath.

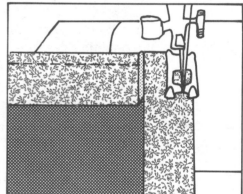

5. Begin sewing 1/4" in from the edge at the original pivot point.

6. Continue stitching and mitering the corners around the outside of the quilt. Avoid seams hitting at corners.

7. End it by overlapping the strip 1/2" at the beginning point.

8. Trim off the excess.

9. Trim the batting and backing up to the raw edge of the binding.

Turning the Binding to the Back

1. Fold the binding to the back side of the quilt.

2. Pin in place so that the folded edge on the binding covers the stitching line. Tuck in the excess fabric at the miter on the diagonal.

3. From the right side, "stitch in the ditch" around the binding. Use the invisible thread on the right side of the quilt, and a bobbin thread to match the binding on the wrong side of the quilt. Catch the edge of the binding with the stitching.

Pillows and Shams

Making the Pillow Front

1. Make one star block following the instructions on pages 27 - 40.

2. Place one star block on the diagonal in the center of 16" square of batting.

3. Machine quilt around the star.

4. Cut the (2) 6 1/2" medium squares on the diagonal into 4 triangles.

5. Pin two medium triangles right sides together to two opposite sides of the star block through the batting. Let the tips hang over equally on both sides. Stitch. Fold out flat.

6. Pin and sew the remaining two triangles to the remaining two sides of the star block. Fold out flat.

7. Pin and sew the 3" borders to two opposite sides. Trim even. Fold out. Repeat with the two remaining sides.

Making the Mock Double Ruffle for the Pillow

1. Seam the (3) 2 1/2" x 45" light strips into one long strip. Seam the (3) 3 1/2" x 45" dark strips into one long strip. Seam the two long strips together lengthwise.

2. Press the seam toward the dark side. Fold and press the long strip in half lengthwise with wrong sides together. On the front side of the ruffle, you will have a 1/2" border of the dark along the folded side.

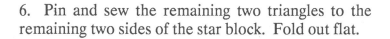

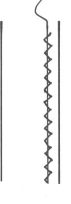

3. Seam the short ends so the strip is one continuous circle.

4. On the back side of the ruffle, lay a string or crochet thread 1/4" from the raw edge. Zigzag over the string being careful not to catch the string.

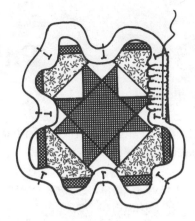

5. Fold the strip into 8 equal parts. Mark each with a pin. Pin the ruffle right sides together to the pillow front, matching the middle and corner of each side. Working on 1/8 of the ruffle at a time, draw up the cord, space the gathers evenly, pin, and stitch.

Finishing the Pillow

1. Place the front of the pillow right sides together to the back. Trim backing to fit.

2. Stitch around the outside edge, leaving a 6" opening in the middle of one side. Turn right side out.

3. Slip the extra piece of batting into the inside of the pillow. Push the corners of the batting into the corners of the pillow. Stuff inbetween the two layers of batting. (Pieces of batting trimmed from the quilt can be shredded and used for stuffing.) Whipstitch the opening shut.

Making Two Pillow Shams

1. Using three star blocks and three chain blocks per sham, sew them together three blocks across and two blocks down. Follow the instructions on pages 48 - 50.

2. First Border: Add the 1 1/2" medium strips to the two short sides. Trim even and fold them out. Add medium strips to the two long sides. Trim and fold them out.

3. Second Border: Add the 2 1/2" dark strips to the shams in the same manner.

4. Place the 3 1/2" wide pregathered lace right sides together to the sham, beginning in the middle of one side. Fold the edge of the lace back 1/2". Baste the lace around the outside of the sham. Overlap the lace at the last 1/2" and trim.

5. Measure the width of the sham. Cut the backing that width by 45". Cut the backing in half down the middle fold.

6. On the selvage edges, fold back a 4" hem, press, and stitch.

7. Lay one backing piece right sides together to the sham, matching the outside edges and placing the hem near the center. Lay the second backing piece on top, overlapping at the center. Pin and stitch around the outside edge. Turn sham right side out.

Acknowledgements

Front Cover Quilt by Eleanor Burns. Double bed quilt with Four Patch Borders. Lightweight Batting. Machine quilted with nylon thread.

Back Cover Quilt by Patricia Knoechel. Twin bed quilt with pink and blue stars in "barnraising" design. Substituted chain blocks for corners on border. Lightweight Batting. Machine quilted with nylon thread.

Front Inside Cover Quilts by Eleanor Burns and Barbara Bredeweg. Lap Robe Quilts with Two-colored Stars. Heavy Batting. Blocks tied and borders "stitched in the ditch."

Back Inside Cover Quilts by Eleanor Burns. Double and Baby quilt with Four Patch Corners. Lightweight Batting. Machine quilted with nylon thread.

A Grateful Thank You to Lucina Heipt for the use of her beautiful home and her creativity in setting up the photos.

Index

Order Information

If you do not have a fine quilt shop in your area, you may write for a complete catalogue of all books and patterns written by Eleanor Burns plus a current price list.

Books , Booklets, and Patterns by Eleanor Burns

Quilt in a Day
Trio of Treasured Quilts
    (Monkey Wrench, Ohio Star, Bear's Paw)
The Sampler, A Machine Sewn Quilt
Lover's Knot
An Amish Quilt in a Day (Roman Stripe)
Irish Chain in a Day
May Basket
Morning Star Quilt
Country Christmas Sewing
Bunnies & Blossoms

Schoolhouse Wallhanging
Diamond Log Cabin Tablecloth and Treeskirt
Log Cabin Christmas Tree Wallhanging
Easy Radiant Star
Country Patchwork Dress
Diamond Vest and Strip Vest
Dresden Plate Placemats and Tea Cozy

Videos for Rent or Purchase by Eleanor Burns

Log Cabin Quilt
Monkey Wrench Quilt
Ohio Star Quilt
Bear's Paw Quilt
Lover's Knot Quilt
Amish Quilt
Schoolhouse Wallhanging

Other Videos

Radiant Star Wallhanging with Jan Donner
Creating With Color with Patricia Knoechel
Victorian Doll with elinore peace bailey

Ask for these at your local public library or video rental store.

Quilt in a Day
1955 Diamond Street, Unit A
San Marcos, Ca. 92069
Order Line: 1-800-24-KWILT   (1-800-245-9458)
CA Orders and Information: 1-(619)-471-7019

If you are ever in San Diego County, southern California, drop by the Quilt in a Day Center with quilt shop and classroom in the La Costa Meadows Business Park. Write ahead for a current class schedule and map.